NORTHERN EUROPE

Cultures and Costumes Series:

CULTURES AND COSTUMES: SYMBOLS OF THEIR PERIOD

NORTHERN EUROPE

EMMA FISCHEL

MASON CREST PUBLISHERS

www.masoncrest.com

Mason Crest Publishers Inc.
370 Reed Road
Broomall, PA 19008
(866) MCP-BOOK (toll free)
www.masoncrest.com

First printing 2002

1 2 3 4 5 6 7 8 9 10

Library of Congress Cataloging-in-Publication Data available

ISBN 1-59084-439-4

Printed and bound in Malaysia

Editorial and design by
Amber Books Ltd.
Bradley's Close
74–77 White Lion Street
London N1 9PF

Project Editor: Marie-Claire Muir
Designer: Hawes Design
Picture Research: Lisa Wren

Picture Credits:
All pictures courtesy of Amber Books Ltd, except the following:
Popperfoto: 8.

ACKNOWLEDGMENT
For authenticating this book, the Publishers would like to thank
Robert L. Humphrey, Jr., Professor Emeritus of Anthropology,
George Washington University, Washington, D.C.

Contents

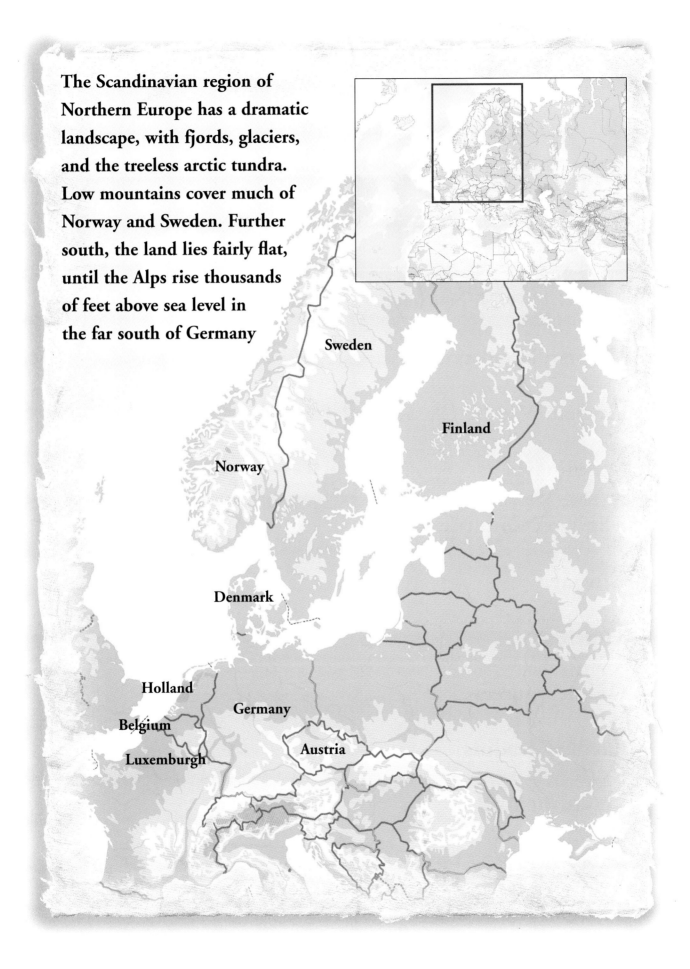

The Scandinavian region of
Northern Europe has a dramatic
landscape, with fjords, glaciers,
and the treeless arctic tundra.
Low mountains cover much of
Norway and Sweden. Further
south, the land lies fairly flat,
until the Alps rise thousands
of feet above sea level in
the far south of Germany

Sweden

Finland

Norway

Denmark

Holland

Germany

Belgium

Luxemburgh

Austria

Introduction

Nearly every species in the animal kingdom adapts to changes in the environment. To cope with cold weather, the cat adapts by growing a longer coat of fur, the bear hibernates, and birds migrate to a different climatic zone. Only humans use costume and culture—what they have learned through many generations—to adapt to the environment.

The first humans developed their culture by using spears to hunt the bear, knives and scrapers to skin it, and needles and sinew to turn the hide into a warm coat to insulate their hairless bodies. As time went on, the clothes humans wore became an indicator of cultural and individual differences. Some were clearly developed to be more comfortable in the environment, others were designed for decorative, economic, political, and religious reasons.

Ritual costumes can tell us about the deities, ancestors, and civil and military ranking in a society, while other clothing styles can identify local or national identity. Social class, gender, age, economic status, climate, profession, and political persuasion are also reflected in clothing. Anthropologists have even tied changes in the hemline length of women's dresses to periods of cultural stress or relative calm.

In 13 beautifully illustrated volumes, the *Cultures and Costumes: Symbols of their Period* series explores the remarkable variety of costumes found around the world and through different eras. Each book shows how different societies have clothed themselves, revealing a wealth of diverse and sometimes mystifying explanations. Costume can be used as a social indicator by scientists, artists, cinematographers, historians, and designers—and also provide students with a better understanding of their own and other cultures.

ROBERT L. HUMPHREY, JR., Professor Emeritus of Anthropology,
George Washington University, Washington, D.C.

The Mighty Norsemen

The northernmost part of Europe, which we now call Scandinavia, was once home to a group of people known as Norsemen. These people, also known as Vikings, lived mainly in the areas now called Norway, Sweden, and Denmark.

At first, the Norsemen were farmers and merchants, but by the time of the late eighth century A.D., that had changed. It was around A.D. 750 when the kings and chieftains of the Norse lands began to gather armies together and launch the first of a long series of terrifying sea raids on other parts of Europe.

The Norse sea raiders were pirates and robbers, brave but ruthless warriors who arrived in huge fleets of mighty warships. They took what they wanted from other lands, looting treasures and taking captives all over Europe and beyond. Many were volunteers, eager to follow their kings and chieftains to conquer new lands. Some men owned little at home. They had no land and not many possessions. Others were **mercenaries**, professional fighters that kings or chieftains paid to protect them, or that merchants paid to protect

The light and slender design of the Norse longships allowed them to sail in close to sloping beaches or up narrow rivers when the Norsemen wanted to make surprise attacks on their enemies.

their cargoes. The raiding expeditions offered a chance of change, adventure, and treasure.

The Norsemen were skilled and savage fighters. They fought armies bigger than their own, attacking suddenly and without mercy. They were feared all over Europe. The reign of terror of these mighty Norse sea raiders continued for over 250 years.

Shipbuilding

The Norsemen were a seafaring race. The rivers, lakes, **fjords**, and the long coastlines made travel by water the obvious way to get around. Ships were an essential part of the Norse way of life, in peace or in war.

The Norsemen built canoes, fishing boats, and ferries. They also built a special type of merchant ship, called a *knorr*, which carried up to 40 people and had a large space in the middle for cargo. However, the Norse shipbuilders were especially famed—and feared—for their mighty longships, the Norse warships. By A.D. 800, Norse shipbuilders had developed a new technique of shipbuilding, and the longships were among the finest ships of that time. Also called dragon ships, they were usually made of oak. Huge and strong, they had billowing sails and long rows of oars down each side. The biggest could have 70 pairs of oars—yet the ships were light and slender, and the crew could carry it if need be. They were fast and nimble, too, and easy to maneuver in battle. The Norsemen gave them names, such as *Long Serpent* and *Wave Walker*.

Work Wear

Not all Norsemen were sea raiders. Some were merchants and traders who did business with other lands and lived in the few towns that had built up as seaports. Many more lived and worked in farming communities.

Farmland was not easy to come by in the Norse lands. To the west, stretched rugged mountains; to the east, dense forests. To the north, were the bleak lands inside the Arctic Circle.

The Norsemen lived in little settlements huddled wherever they could find patches of fertile land to farm, mainly around the lakes and fjords in the south. In summer, the days were long and light, but winters were bitterly cold, with few hours of daylight. The sun barely rose above the horizon, the temperatures plummeted, and fierce blizzards swept in and covered the whole of the Norse lands in snow.

The Norsemen were not just farmers, they were also hunters and fishermen. They used bows and arrows, traps, and spears. They hunted foxes and otters, deer and wild boar; they tracked great bears through the forests. They also caught salmon, herring, and cod, sometimes seals and walruses, and even great whales, which they drove onto the beaches and killed.

Clothes had to be warm, tough, protective, and easy to move in. An ordinary Norseman would dress in a long-sleeved linen shirt. His trousers were probably made of wool. Sometimes, the legs were left straight; sometimes, they were tied with pieces of cloth. A **drawstring** pulled the trousers tight around the waist.

In winter, a Norseman wore a **tunic** belted over the top. The belt was leather and had a purse or a knife hanging from it. Over that, he wore a heavy woolen cloak or furs.

A warrior would pin his cloak over one shoulder with a cloak pin. That way, his sword arm was free to lash out at his enemies.

Poor people's clothes were made of coarse cloth and left plain and undyed. The rich had finer cloth, dyed in strong colors. They might have decorated cuffs, hem, and neckline, made with bright woven bands of patterned cloth. They might even have clothes decorated with gold and silver thread or silks from China for feasts and special occasions.

Women wore long dresses with a tunic of linen or wool over the top. The dresses were sometimes pleated and fastened around the neck with a drawstring or **brooch**. The sleeves were long or short.

The tunic was made of two rectangles of material joined at the shoulder by straps. Women used brooches to fasten the straps to the tunic. Some tunics were made brighter by weaving bands of material through them. Women also wore shawls, and in cold weather, some had cloaks with linings made of seabird feathers.

Some women hung a little chain from one of the tunic brooches and attached useful things to the

Clothes had to adapt easily to the changing seasons, with extra layers added in the harsh winters. Hats could be made of fur, wool, or leather.

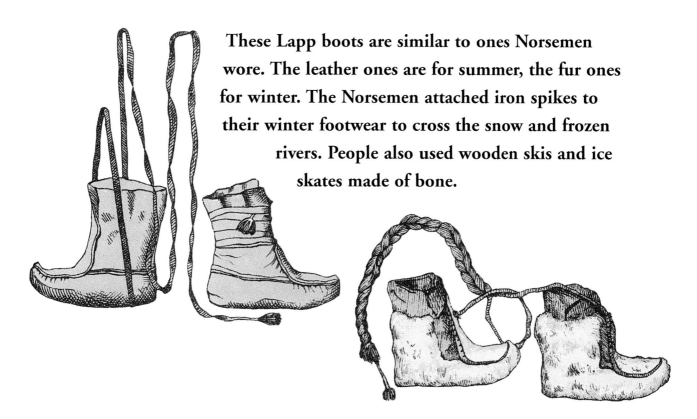

These Lapp boots are similar to ones Norsemen wore. The leather ones are for summer, the fur ones for winter. The Norsemen attached iron spikes to their winter footwear to cross the snow and frozen rivers. People also used wooden skis and ice skates made of bone.

chain—perhaps a knife or some scissors, or a comb carved out of bone and red-deer antler, sometimes even in its own little case. She might carry her house keys and even keys to chests filled with precious silks or jewels.

Men and women all wore shoes and boots, usually made of leather, that fastened around the ankles.

Beards and Braids, Bands and Baubles

Most Norsemen wore beards. Some trimmed their beards into a fork shape, others braided them. Overall, men kept their hair around shoulder length, although some warriors grew it longer. Some braided their hair or beards to keep them out of the way while they were hunting or fighting. Others tied a band around their forehead for the same reason.

Women grew their hair long and either braided it or tied it in a knot on top of their heads. Or, they might tie patterned bands around their foreheads. Married women covered their hair with a head scarf.

The Norse people were skilled in making jewelry, and they wore a lot of it.

Even belt buckles were intricately worked and shaped. In particular, they liked metal ornaments. They wore heavy rings, called torques, around their necks. They also wore rings and armlets—warriors were sometimes paid in armlets.

Tunic brooches for women came in all types of shapes and a variety of decorations. Some were oval; some round and decorated with silver wire. They might have patterns of spirals or depict stylized animals. Between the tunic brooches, many women strung beads. These could be pottery, **amber**, glass, or crystal. Many people also wore **amulets** to bring them good fortune.

Norse Jewelry

The rich wore gold and silver and had their jewelry individually made. Poorer people had to make do with jewelry that was cast in iron, bronze, or copper.

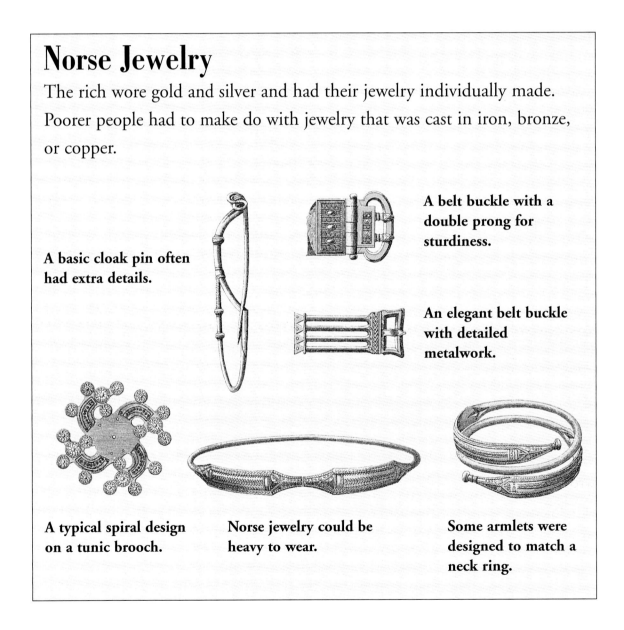

A belt buckle with a double prong for sturdiness.

A basic cloak pin often had extra details.

An elegant belt buckle with detailed metalwork.

A typical spiral design on a tunic brooch.

Norse jewelry could be heavy to wear.

Some armlets were designed to match a neck ring.

How Do We Know What the Norsemen Wore?

Archaeologists have uncovered Norse burial graves that tell us a lot about their way of life. Richer Norsemen were buried surrounded by all the things that had been most meaningful to them. A warrior was buried with his sword, for example, a merchant with his weighing scales, a farmer with his tools. There might also be favorite pieces of jewelry, or even a much-loved horse or dog. However, clothes have been harder to find, because they disintegrate over time. Even so, some pieces of clothing have survived, preserved in boggy ground, and further scraps have been found in burial mounds.

Pictures can tell a lot about what people wore. The Norse people sometimes set up stone monuments in memory of their loved ones, and these would have images carved on them. Tapestries, too, would show scenes of Norse events. Tales of the brave deeds of the Norsemen were passed on orally from father to son, generation after generation, and were eventually written down. Sometimes, these gave clues to the clothes and styles they wore. All these things pieced together provide a good idea of what the Norsemen wore.

Warriors and Weapons

Warriors wore much the same clothes as other Norsemen, and then added whatever protective clothing and armor they could. The richer professional warriors wore a *byrnie*, a chain mail shirt reaching to the hips or knees. It was strong enough to make it difficult for enemy weapons to pierce. It was also expensive, because it consisted of thousands of handmade iron rings all interlocked, so it was often handed down from father to son through many generations. Unluckier men had to make do with padded leather jackets to protect them.

Helmets were usually leather or metal. They might be round or **conical**, and many had a straight piece coming down to protect the nose. Experts do not think they were decorated with wings and horns, although many pictures show them that way.

One group of Norse warriors liked to prove how brave they were by fighting without any armor at all. Called *berserks*, they were known for their savage fighting and wild ways. Before a battle, they would shout out insulting speeches about their enemies and boast about their own skill and bravery.

The Norse fighters used all types of weapons. Some had wooden bows and metal-tipped arrows. Many used an ax. Norse axes were huge and heavy, with a long wooden shaft and a rounded iron blade. Some of them were decorated with silver wire.

Spears, again made in iron and wood, came in two weights, and most warriors carried both. The lighter javelin spear was for hurling at the enemy. The heavier, longer spear was for thrusting when the enemy was near enough for hand-to-hand fighting.

Warriors kept knives in leather sheaths, and swords in **scabbards** made of wood or leather. Swords had sharp blades on both edges. They were flexible, yet strong, and made of iron rods twisted together and beaten flat, which made them hard to break.

Warriors carried shields that were big enough to cover them from chin to knee. They were round and wooden with a metal rim. The warrior's hand was protected by a metal cap, called a boss, in the middle of the shield. Some shields had pictures or patterns on them.

Norse Gods and Beliefs

The Norsemen worshipped many types of gods and goddesses. Chief of them all was Odin, king of the gods and ruler of all things. Odin was the god of battle. He hurled his magic spear down at the human world and caused all the wars on earth. He had only one eye and rode on a mighty eight-legged horse

Armed and Dangerous

Warriors greatly treasured their swords, which were expensive and often highly decorated. Warriors gave their swords names, such as *Legbiter* or *Adder*.

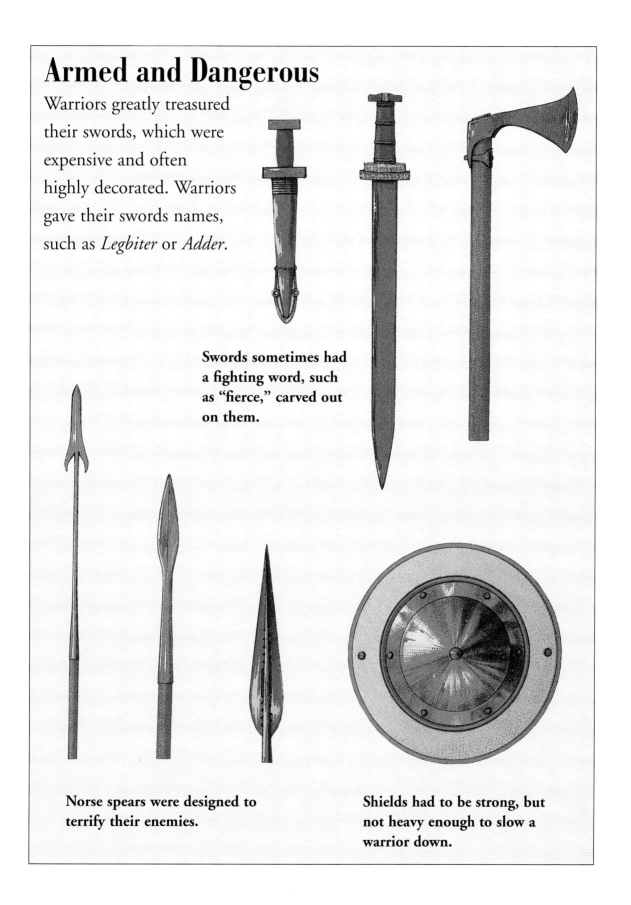

Swords sometimes had a fighting word, such as "fierce," carved out on them.

Norse spears were designed to terrify their enemies.

Shields had to be strong, but not heavy enough to slow a warrior down.

called Sleipnir. On each of his shoulders sat a raven. One was called Thought, one Memory. They would fly around the world every day and tell Odin what they saw. The middle day of the week, Wednesday, is derived from his name in Old English, Woden.

Thor, the god of law and order, had flaming red hair and beard and loved feasting, drinking, and fighting. He hurtled through the skies in a chariot pulled by huge goats, wielding his magic hammer called Mjollnir, which he used without mercy on his enemies. Thursday is named for this god.

Norsemen also believed that the universe was made up of different levels. Midgard was the middle level, the human world. Above it, and connected by a flaming rainbow bridge called Bifrost, was Asgard, the place where the gods lived. The lowest level contained two lands. One was Niflheim, the land of the dead, a place of ice and darkness. The other was Muspelheim, a land of fire.

Childhood

Norse children did not have the luxury of their own room. In fact, few people did. A house in a town or one belonging to a chieftain might have two or three rooms. However, a child in a farming community often lived in a one-room

Baby Boom?

Many historians think the reason the Norsemen took to raiding other lands was because there was a baby boom in their own lands. By the end of the eighth century A.D., the Norsemen had built up strong farming communities and good trade links with other parts of the world. Success at home and abroad meant that the population began to grow—but there was no more good land to farm. Farmers were forced onto land where the soil was poor and crops grew badly. Faced with starvation, they began to raid other lands and find new places to settle and farm.

building, a long rectangular room called a hall. Everyone ate, slept, and lived in it together. In winter, the farm animals were kept in there as well, in an enclosure at one end of the room. The animals helped make the room warmer. There was not much furniture in Norse times—long benches covered in furs, a table, some storage barrels, but not much more.

Cooking went on inside the hall, over a big fire in the middle of the room—this could be hazardous, considering that the houses were usually made of wood, with thatched roofs. Norse children could not afford to be picky about food. Fish and porridge were often on the menu.

There was no formal schooling, but every child learned basic skills from an early age. Boys hunted and handled weapons, and they learned to farm and to sail, to carve and to work metal. Sons of traders might go on long sea voyages.

Girls learned to cook, to bake bread, and to care for babies. However, most important of all, they learned to make cloth. Spinning and weaving took up a large part of a woman's day. Women had to make clothes for the whole household, and dye them with vegetables and minerals. They made blankets and tapestries, too, and even sails for the fleets of mighty Norse boats.

In Norse times, the oldest son inherited whatever land or property the family had when the father died. Younger sons, left with nothing, often became professional warriors or joined raiding parties to find riches abroad.

German Nobility

Up until the late 19th century, Germany was made up of separate states, or kingdoms, all of which had their own rulers. All those kingdoms were, in turn, ruled over by the powerful Hapsburg family of Austria.

The Catholic Hapsburgs provided Germany with emperors until the beginning of the 19th century, but not without struggles. In the 16th century, new Protestant religious ideas spread from Saxony to other German states. These states quarreled with the emperor and eventually fought for the right to choose their own state's religion. They succeeded in 1555.

Courtly Copycats

Fashions have always changed according to the times people live in. In good times, the creators of new looks are perhaps more drawn to brighter colors or more relaxed shapes. In bad times, they may move toward shapes that are more rigid, bleaker outlines, and darker colors.

In centuries gone by, those changes in style—changes to the length or shape of a sleeve, or changes to styles of wearing hair, or the adding of a **bustle** to a dress, or even a radical change to the shape of the dress—nearly always got their start in the courts of royalty.

The emperor, pictured above, holds a globe with a cross on top, symbolizing the Christian church. The doctor, pictured below, wears a long cloak; the courtiers, short ones.

All over Europe, the different courts in France, Spain, Italy, and elsewhere were experimenting with fashions and influencing each other. Courts had a lot of contact with each other, so new styles spread quickly.

These fashion styles filtered down to the less wealthy, possibly in a more restrained version, certainly in coarser materials, and probably years behind. Throughout time, the nobility had tried to prevent the less-privileged from dressing in any way that resembled those in exclusive court circles. It was ironic, then, that when it was Germany's turn to influence the style of male dress in courts all over Europe, the fashion came from German mercenaries.

Slashing

Slashing was a way of showing the material that lined a garment by cutting slits in the top material and pulling the lining through. The basic idea came from German mercenaries, or *landsknecht*, who themselves had gotten the idea from Swiss soldiers. The story went that the Swiss, a ragged bunch of soldiers, had celebrated a victory by slashing the fine silks of their enemies and using them to patch their own clothes. The German *landsknecht* used the idea to develop their own form of slashing. Soon, the idea was copied by German nobles.

It did not take long for slashing to spread from the German court to the French court. The French king was married to the English king's sister, so the English court was slashing, too. Soon after that, slashing spread across Europe.

The Germans took slashing to the extreme. They slashed almost everything, using vast amounts of fabric. They slashed **doublets** and breeches, with the slashing sometimes being different on each leg or sleeve. The lining might be of a different pattern or another color. Even their shoes and their hat brims did not escape slashing. Women's clothes were slashed, too, but not as much.

Color Change

In the first half of the 16th century, the German nobility led the way in using rich, bright colors in their clothes. Women's clothes were more restrained

Bombast could be made of all types of materials—rag, horsehair, flock, cotton, even bran. Bran had its drawbacks if the cloth was torn—it spilled straight out.

than men's, but they were richly embroidered. They wore gowns, tightly fitted at the waist, and falling in big folds to the ground, over a **kirtle**. Sleeves grew wider and wider, with a deep fur cuff. Fur, especially lynx, wolf, and sable, was used to trim both men's and women's clothes.

Male fashions were flamboyant. The main garment was a jacket called a doublet, which might reach down to the knees. Some had an opening in the front where the **codpiece** showed through. Others might have double sleeves, with one pair hanging loose and in a different color. Doublets were made of rich materials in rich colors—blue velvet, perhaps, lined with **cloth of gold**. Red, too, was much favored by the nobility. Over the doublet, nobles wore a jacket or **jerkin**, and over that a gown, usually edged with fur.

Hats for men were usually a soft, low bonnet, sometimes with a brim that could be turned up in front and kept in place by a jewel. Again, hats came in rich, bright materials, such as velvet, satin, and cloth of gold.

Embroidery was on everything, and so were jewels—from hats to shoes and everything in between. On some clothes, the material was invisible, hidden by the diamonds, rubies, and pearls attached to its surface.

In the mid-16th century, when the Spanish court began to dominate

In the late 17th century, men's clothes began to evolve into what we now call a suit. The long jacket was often left undone and flared out. Cravats of lace or muslin were worn, and sleeves had deep cuffs.

fashion, the flamboyant style began to disappear. Bright colors gave way to black and somber shades, and flowing fashions gave way to fitted, more rigid ones from the more formal Spanish court.

Special Effects

Men and women have been willing to suffer for fashion throughout the ages. In the 16th century, bombast was one of the culprits. Bombast was stuffing used in doublets and hose. The idea was to fill them out to get rid of any creases or folds. Filling them out in this way also made the waist appear smaller, and tight lacing then completed the effect.

Around this time, knitting was also introduced, which meant a much smoother leg line was possible than before. This came in useful, as bombasted breeches left a lot of leg exposed.

Women suffered, too, from hoops worn under skirts. The farthingale was a Spanish invention, which was then modified by the French and others. It was a structure made of hoops that formed an expanded framework for the skirt to drape over. The Spanish farthingale, made of wire, wood, or whalebone, was a bell shape, growing bigger toward the bottom. The French came up with a farthingale shaped like a wheel, and the wearer stood in the middle of it. This meant that the skirt went out, then dramatically straight down.

Hoops returned to fashion in the 18th century, but now they projected out sideways, sometimes as much as 15 feet (3 m), which made most maneuvers extremely difficult. It was impossible for two women to pass through a door side by side, or even to sit on the same couch.

Later in that century, the crinoline improved things. This was a more flexible steel structure and gave skirts fullness that would otherwise have needed six petticoats to achieve.

Wigs

Wigs were an essential fashion accessory in the 17th century. The French king, Louis XIV, introduced the first one, which was known as the periwig. It was full and long, a mass of curls falling to below the shoulders, sometimes almost to

Fashion, Furniture, and Art

There is a strong link between styles in clothes and styles in furniture. When dresses got wider, furniture designers began to make chairs without arms, or with arms that spread outward. When the fashion was for high headdresses or big wigs, chairs started to be made with higher backs.

In the same way, fashion influenced painting. Many court portraits were painted in the 16th century all over Europe. Art historians have noticed how the type of fashion influenced the painter and the way he chose to paint his subject. For instance, when courts adopted the more formal Spanish style, abandoning the bright, flowing colors of before, that feeling of formality was echoed in paintings. Men are shown standing upright and stiff, with one foot stretched straight forward and their heads held high and rigid.

These are all variations on the periwig. The choice of wig depended on age and profession, as well as personal preference. The magistrate in the middle wears a more extreme version of the periwig.

the waist. To make a periwig fit properly, men had to cut their hair close to the scalp, or even shave it. Wigs were expensive and heavy. Men in active professions, such as soldiers or laborers, could not possibly wear one. That exclusivity was much appreciated in certain circles. In court circles, a wig was considered essential for nearly a century, and many other styles of wig soon followed the periwig. The wigs were not made of only human hair. The hair might have been taken from horses, cows, goats, or foxes. They could be covered in powder of various shades—white, gray, blue, brown, or black. Women did not generally wear wigs, although they might add false curls at the back of the head.

Hair and Headdresses

In the 1690s, a new hairstyle was created. Called the *fontange*, a favorite guest at the French court of Louis XIV invented it. She had been out with a hunting party, and her hair had become disheveled and loose. Thinking quickly, she tied it up using one of her garters. Louis XIV greatly admired the effect, and by the

The Must-Haves

There were several accessories that the well-dressed lady or gentleman of the German court did not want to be without. In the first half of the 16th century, for example, men wore gauntlet-style gloves with elaborately embroidered cuffs.

Ladies and gentlemen in the 17th century had bows, ribbons, straps, buttons, and buckles attached to everything. Snuff was carried in a beautifully carved snuffbox (both men and women used snuff until the early 19th century). Ladies wore a hand-cut comb in bone or ivory with intricately carved details; and they used a folding fan, with a specially commissioned scene painted on it. (Fans were a new arrival in Europe, but in China, they had already been used for over 500 years.)

In the 18th century, **beauty spots** were worn by everyone. They were cut into shapes, such as moons, stars, suns, and hearts. Little ivory claws on the end of a long stick were used by ladies to relieve itching caused by the small creatures living in their huge headdresses.

next day, all the women at the court had adopted it—with ribbons and a bow in front replacing the garter. However, the *fontange* did not stop there. Soon, women added lace to it, then a cap with a wire frame to keep it in place. The frame was then made higher and covered in thin silks, building the hair up into a high peak crowned by a high cap.

More and more elaborate experiments with hair continued in the 18th century. Hair was pulled and strained over cushions, or forced into elaborate shapes over wire frames that stayed in place for months. Headdresses became like works of art. On top of her head, a woman might have a ship in full sail or a windmill and farm animals. They reached so high that chandelier candles posed a serious fire risk to them.

German Middle Classes and Trades

In the Middle Ages, most people in Germany worked on the land. They made their own clothes in simple tunic and dress shapes. Even for the rich, the only materials were wool, linen, and leather, and dyes were made from plants or from earth.

The Crusades, Christian Europe's wars against the Muslim East, brought about changes in many areas of life, including what people wore. Soldiers went off to fight from all over Europe, and Germany played a big part. In the lands of the East, they discovered new, rich materials, such as **damask** and **gauze**, and brought them back to Germany.

By this time, small groups of merchants and craftsmen were emerging in the small towns that existed. Over the next century, the towns became larger, and so did

These men and women are from various trade guilds. Headgear for women was varied. The seated woman on the left, pictured above, wears a simple cloth surrounding her face, while the one on the right wears a round hat made of otter skin.

the groups of merchants and craftsmen. They were not rich or privileged, like the nobles. They were not poor or downtrodden, like the peasants. They formed a new middle level, somewhere in between, of hardworking, more prosperous citizens.

As the 16th century began, German towns continued to grow, fast becoming cities. The numbers of new middle-class city folk were also growing. Known as *burghers*, they made money from mining, banking, and trading, and they dressed to suit their middle-class status in life.

One thing every well-to-do *burgher* had was a *schaube*, a long overcoat, generally without sleeves. If it did have sleeves, they were not used. They hung empty behind the sleeves of the garment underneath. The *schaube* was often lined with fur and lent an air of dignity to its wearer. It was particularly popular with scholars.

Sumptuary Laws

Middle-class garments did not have any of the extravagance of those worn in

The Christmas Tree Legend

The tradition of bringing a tree indoors and decorating it for Christmas first began as a German tradition. Legend has it that Martin Luther is responsible for starting the fashion. According to the story, Luther was walking through a snow-covered forest one Christmas Eve. He was so affected by the beauty of the snowy evergreens lit by starlight that he cut down a small fir. He took it home and placed lighted candles on the boughs so that his wife and children might see the heavenly light that had dazzled him.

Because of its rumored associations with Luther, the strongly Catholic parts of the south refused to have a tree as part of their Christmas celebrations until the late 19th century.

Many middle-class women wore a *kittel* (a jacket with a little cape fitted over it and fur-trimmed sleeves) and a *pelzkappe* (a round fur hat). The woman on the right has an elaborate hairstyle under her *pelzkappe*.

court circles—but they were not supposed to. For centuries, the nobility all over Europe had been making sumptuary laws. These were laws that said what clothes the different groups of people in society were allowed to wear. For example, a king might say that no one below the rank of a noble could wear velvet, satin, or silk.

As populations got bigger and new groups of people got wealthier, the nobles saw that such distinctions between different groups were becoming less clear. Sumptuary laws were a way of preserving these distinctions by trying to make sure everyone understood who was more important than whom.

Sumptuary laws could be quite detailed. They could specify the length of shoe or the particular quality of cloth different groups should have. One early law divided men into five different classes, or *stande*, then went on to detail exactly what the wives of each class of man should wear.

These laws gave details of the fines to be paid for disobeying them—

The coat of this Protestant minister has little pleats and puffed sleeves. This costume, but not the hat, is what Luther would have worn when he became a professor of theology.

however, they did not prove successful in any of the countries that had adopted them, and Germany was no exception. In spite of the laws, the middle classes imitated the nobles as much as they dared.

A Nation Divided: Germany and Religion

Religion has always had a big influence on fashion, and in the past, it was often possible to tell the faith of a person from his clothes. Until the early 16th century, Germany was a Catholic country, with the Catholic Hapsburgs ruling over all the princes in the different states. Then a man named Martin Luther began to spread his ideas about religion, and everything changed.

A monk and a professor of theology, Luther began to criticize certain practices in the Catholic Church. He was angry with how it was run and the way it taught people about religious beliefs. In 1517, he nailed a list of his ideas for making it better to the door of a church in Germany.

The leaders of the Catholic Church were furious, and Luther had to go into hiding for the next few years. However, by 1525, he had organized his own church, the Lutheran Church, based on new Protestant beliefs and practices. It became the official religion of Saxony in the north of Germany and quickly spread to other northern and central German states.

For more than a century afterward, there was great division between Protestants and Catholics in Germany. This turmoil eventually led to the Thirty Years War, a savage conflict in which up to one in three Germans died. After that, the two religions managed to coexist peacefully, with most Protestants living in the north and Catholics residing in the south.

In general, the Protestants were more restrained in their dress, wearing dark, somber colors, plain styles, and black hats. Jewelry and unnecessary ornamentation were frowned upon. Catholics' clothes were brighter. They wore colorful yellow hats with green ribbons, and styles that were more flamboyant.

The Guilds

The merchants and craftsmen of the early Middle Ages started forming associations called guilds. The idea was to establish sets of rules for each trade—about what prices they could charge, wages they could pay, conditions for their workers, standards for work and trade, and care for members in trouble.

Housewarming

As cities grew and the middle classes became more numerous, new houses were built and a tradition grew up around building houses. As the last roof beam was secured in place, it was time to celebrate. In the north, they hung up a wreath called a *richtkrone*, and in the south, a decorated bush. Then the new owner gave a party.

Sometimes, friends or neighbors took the last beam away before it was secured in place and carved beautiful decorations on it. Once the beam was in place, one of the carpenters would stand on the roof and give thanks to God. He would ask for blessings on the house and all who were to live in it. Then he drank to the health of the house owner and his family before throwing his glass to the ground. It was considered to bring bad luck if the glass did not smash properly.

Every neighbor gave the new owner something for the house. It might be a carved beam with a colorful motto, or a window painted with a portrait of the house owner and his wife.

The guilds did not always work as well as they should have, and the one run by rich merchants had much more influence with city governments than the guilds of ordinary craftsmen.

No one could trade without belonging to a guild, but before anyone could belong to a guild, he had to train for anywhere between 4 and 11 years. Even then, to join a guild, a man might have to own property of a certain value or pay a fee, and he simply might not be able to meet the requirements.

During the 18th century, various laws were passed to improve things. Even so, riots and strikes went on. In 1793, the army was called in to stop a strike by tailors in which 27 people died.

Men's hats came in a lot of shapes, but all of them had wide brims and were made of black felt, like the one worn by the man in the center. The seated woman's hat with the arched back is held on by straps tied under her chin.

Poverty and Disease

Poverty was a huge problem in the 18th century. Almost a quarter of the population lived below the poverty line. That meant they had less money than they needed for the very basics of life—food, clothes, and shelter. Some of those were *burghers* who had gone bankrupt. Disease was a problem, too. Towns were filthy places, and smallpox was a big killer.

Infant deaths were high. In most families, a child was born every two and a half years, but at least one in three babies died at or near birth. Children died, too, of horrible diseases, such as tuberculosis and typhus. In some places, 7 out of 10 children died before they were 14 years old, and most families had only two children who survived into adulthood.

The Rise of Prussia

By the 18th century, the strongest state in Germany was Prussia, in the Protestant north, whose capital was Berlin. The Prussian army was considered

Theater and Music

There are theaters all over Germany, many of which German princes built in the 17th and 18th centuries. By the 19th century, municipal theaters called *schauspielhaus* were built, paid for by wealthy citizens. Goethe and Schiller, two of the world's greatest playwrights, were both born in the mid-18th century and were writing into the following century.

The 18th and 19th centuries also produced some of the world's finest composers. Among them are Bach and Handel, followed by Beethoven, then Mendelssohn and Schumann.

In earlier times, music was performed only at court or in churches, but in 1722, Hamburg held the first public concert in Germany. Many other cities followed soon afterward. Composers were sponsored by courts and wealthy individuals and, later, by concert promoters.

The officer in the middle is an infantry general. To the left is Prince Henry, Frederick II's brother. To the right is Frederick II. The medal he is wearing is the Order of Military Merit, founded by him in 1744.

Wagner and Bavaria

The composer Richard Wagner lived in Bavaria for more than 10 years. He had written a cycle of four operas, *The Ring of the Nibelung*, which included a variety of dramatic special effects, such as cast members seeming to fly.

Wagner realized that there were no theaters in Bavaria well equipped enough to put on his operas, so he built his own opera house, the Bayreuth Festival Theater. It opened in 1876 with the first performance of *The Ring*. Now, there is a Wagner music festival in Bavaria each year.

one of the best in Europe. It was famous for its discipline and obedience, and its distinctive blue, red, and yellow uniforms were admired and copied throughout Europe. Generally, infantry officers wore the same uniform as their troops. The **insignia** on an officer's hat indicated his rank.

Prussia's most successful king was Frederick II, who was known as Frederick the Great. He ruled from 1740 to 1786. He brought in a fairer legal system, abolished censorship and torture, and declared religious freedom for all

Prussians. Frederick II also made great improvements to education, agriculture, and industry. He worked hard to modernize Prussia and create a strong and efficient government.

At that time, a new body of officials was created, the *beamtentum*. The *beamtentum* were drawn from the middle classes. They were efficient, hardworking, dutiful servants of the ruler in whichever state they lived, but they were not always popular.

Bavarian *Tracht*

Bavaria was an important state in the south of Germany. By the 19th century, it had a reputation as an artistic place and was popular with German writers and painters. It was a region of great beauty, with lakes and **gorges**, the rugged Bavarian Alps to the south, and the Black Forest (Schwarzwald), with its fir and spruce trees, to the west.

The strong, simple outline was achieved only with help from undergarments. A merchant woman, like the one in the middle, would be regarded as poor if she wore less than six petticoats under her skirt.

Great attention was paid to the look of an outfit from the back as well as the front, with elaborate bows and ribbons added at the waist and shoulders, or on the hat.

Bavarian *tracht* is the name given to the clothes worn in the different regions within the state. Women's *tracht* was usually lace caps and *dirndlkleider*, embroidered, close-fitting bodices and full skirts, worn with an apron over the top. The skirts were large, often pleated and starched. Many women wore layers of petticoats underneath to give the skirts even more fullness. Men's *tracht* was *lederhosen* (leather shorts) with knee socks, a shirt, and jacket.

The different clothing reflected the economy of the area. In an area that was mainly a farming community, for example, people would be poor, and the simplicity of their *tracht* reflected that. Of course, a more wealthy area would have more elaborate *tracht*.

The *lederhosen*, worn with knee socks, can be seen on this man. His *tracht* has been completed with a shirt and jacket, along with a traditional hat.

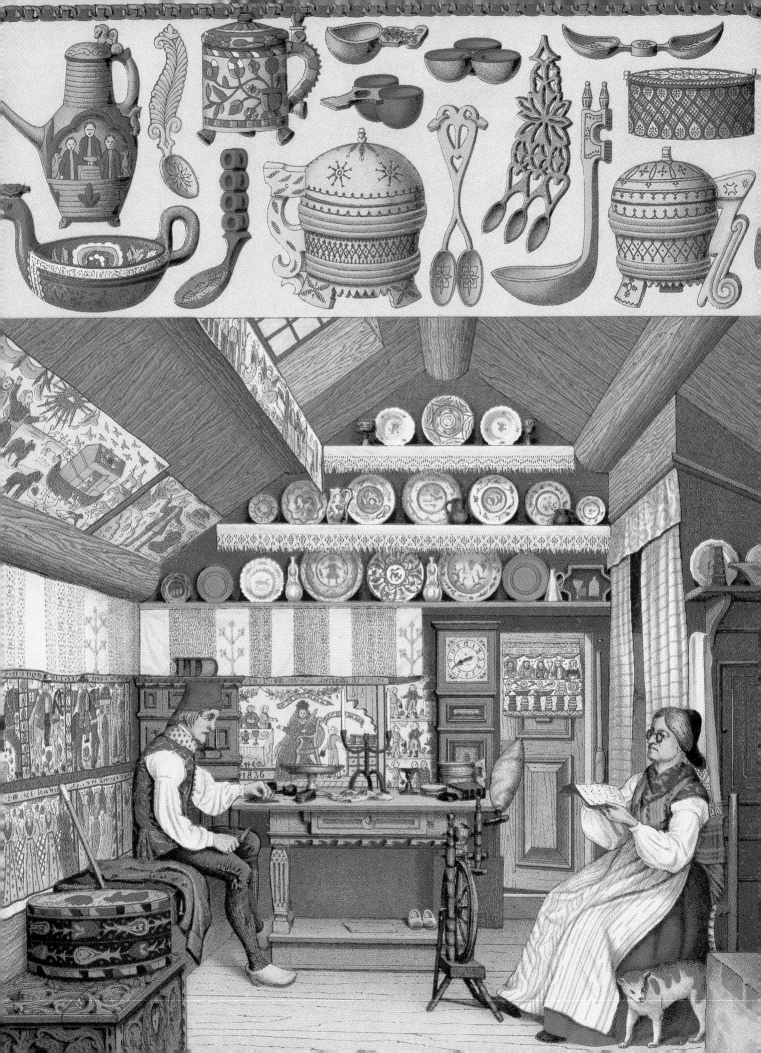

Scandinavia

Down the centuries, the Scandinavians have fought each other, ruled each other, protected each other, and invaded each other. Yet these fiercely independent lands have shared more than borders and history.

The area known as Scandinavia has a history of domination by one people over another. The Swedes ruled the Finns, the Danes ruled the Swedes, the Danes and the Swedes ruled the Norwegians, and so on. However, these people have also been united in their struggles to make a living from their lands so far to the cold north.

Scandinavia—apart from Denmark—stretches up into the Arctic Circle, where the sun never rises between November and February. Even to the south, Scandinavian winters are bitter and long. The mountains and forests mean there are huge areas that are hard to reach. There is not much fertile land, and for centuries, there was not much industry beyond farming and fishing.

By the 19th century, a number of towns had grown up, but even then Scandinavia was still largely made up of tiny communities, widely scattered and remote from each other. They were poor communities. Farmers—eking out a living by fishing and hunting, not traveling far, not meeting people from other places—kept pretty much to themselves.

This room is a typical Scandinavian interior of the late 19th century, with woven wall hangings, plates displayed on wooden shelves, and the spinning wheel forming the centerpiece of the room.

However, it was in these isolated areas that a great folk heritage grew. Strong traditions developed without much outside influence to change them, traditions of music and of dancing, of folk tales and legends—and of costume.

Folk Dress

In the few Scandinavian towns, fashions from other parts of Europe might filter slowly into the styles and shapes the richer people wore, but not in the little communities out in the countryside. People there continued to wear styles that had evolved in their own restricted area. Any influence from the rest of Europe could take decades to reach them.

Folk dress is the term for all the types of clothes that the ordinary people—farmers, miners, fishermen, blacksmiths, and so on—wore up to around the middle of the 19th century. Folk dress could be work clothes, special-occasion clothes, summer clothes, winter clothes, whatever the ordinary people wore in earlier times.

All over Scandinavia, the peasant clothes were made of much the same materials: wool or cotton. They were durable, practical clothes, set off by tough boots or sturdy shoes. There was no money for silks and velvets, but on the special-occasion clothes, there was beautiful embroidery with gold and silver thread, as well as intricate weaving and details.

Each country had a different look. In Denmark, for example, by end of the 17th century, a basic

This Swedish miner is in winter clothes. The coat is in coarse woolen cloth and would be white or black, depending on the district he came from. His strong shoes have two soles.

These people are in their Sunday best. The shape, style, and color of the clothes pinpoints them to a particular mining area. The woman's pointed hat is of black wool with red details.

costume for peasant women had evolved: a headpiece, a blouse with a bodice on top, a skirt with an apron over it, and some kind of neckerchief or scarf. The skirt and **bodice** were made of a heavy fabric, and the skirt would have a large apron over the top in white, black, or blue. Green and red featured a lot, and they are in most Scandinavian costumes. The peasants made most of the dye colors themselves, but blue and red had to be bought.

Caps were always part of the Danish peasant costume, although the shape varied dramatically, depending on which part of the country and which period they came from. They could be small and tight-fitting and worn under another cap, or huge and cone-shaped and wrapped with ribbons. Unmarried girls did not wear them; instead, they wore their hair in braids around their head.

By the 1660s, men wore a shirt, vest, and trousers. The vest grew gradually shorter, and by the early 18th century, it had a high collar and a double row of buttons. The long socks extending to the knee might have bright bands knitted around the top. Many men wore a red wool stocking cap called a *nissehat*.

Folk Tales

It was in these poor rural areas that the great tradition of Scandinavian folk tales developed. Farmers and forest workers told or listened to tales of deep northern forests and enormous, clumsy trolls that turned to stone if they were caught by the rays of the sun.

A Hard Life

It was a hard life in rural areas. Poorest of all were the *husmenn*, Norwegian tenant farmers working tiny farms. There were also many migrant and seasonal workers, including young children. The roads were terrible, and in winter they could be impassable, so people were often isolated. The best forms of transportation in winter were skis or skates, and in summer, boats. Many churches were built on lakes, and people went to church by boat.

Houses were built of wood, so they were warm—but there were many lice and other small pests. Old-fashioned houses in the country had one fireplace in the middle of the room, and the houses were usually filled with smoke.

Food could be scarce in the long, hard winters, but the poor were clever at making food go as far as it could. Meats were smoked and dried to see them through the long, hard winters. Every bit of the animal was used; they even smoked sheep's heads. Swedes and Finns, in particular, were good at drying, preserving, and making use of edible fungi. In Finland, when winters were especially harsh, and also in spring before anything grew, the Finns used to eat bark in their bread.

All Scandinavians picked berries, bottling and preserving them to give them a source of vitamin C in the winter. They used blueberries, cloudberries, and *tyttebar* (red whortleberries, or mountain cranberries). They ate boiled potatoes and porridge made with oats and flour. A big treat was *rommegrot*, made with sour cream.

Tales were told of young men imprisoned in the mountains, lured there by the *hulder*, beautiful country girls with long, fair hair. The young men were so enchanted by the beauty of the *hulder* that they failed to see the girls all had a cow's tail. Other tales told of mossy forest glades and of *nisse*, small people with long gray beards and red wooly hats who helped or hindered farmers according to how the farmers treated them.

Swedish *Folkdrakt*

Many areas developed their own kinds of costume, which were further variations on the general costume of that country. In Sweden, the term *folkdrakt* is used to mean a locally distinct costume.

Many communities were in places with natural boundaries that made it hard for the world outside to intrude, perhaps a river or mountains or a forest. Inside such areas, there developed a way of dressing that showed the people's own local character.

The same was happening in other Scandinavian countries. Norway had even more isolated communities of small farms and fishing hamlets, clinging to the sides of fjords and rocky coastal islands on the west. Here, as in Sweden, everyone would be using the same locally produced materials, and anything that came in from outside was also used by everyone.

Sometimes, a shoemaker or tailor, or his customer, could get into trouble for trying a new way of doing

This woman is from Iceland, an island of glaciers and volcanoes. She is wearing a ceremonial feast costume. Colors were always somber and muted, sometimes black.

Fish, Fowl, and Four-Legged Food

The Scandinavians ate fish in every form. In the north, they had *klipfisk*, cod dried in the sun. *Lutefisk*, cod soaked in lye, still survives as a dish among people of Norwegian descent.

Herring was a staple dish. If a large shoal of herring filled the bay, the peasants called it "the silver of the sea." Salmon were plentiful in rivers and seas. In fact, in some of the wealthier houses, it was put on the table so often that the servants had a contract to say they would not have to eat salmon every day.

Game was plentiful, too, particularly elk, reindeer, and ptarmigan (a type of grouse). There is a lot of "common" land in Scandinavia. In Norway, for example, the land belongs to everyone. Anyone is free to net, snare, shoot, or fish.

things. They could be fined for producing a change in the traditional style of that community—or even put into the **stocks** outside the church as a warning to others.

On the Move

In the mid-19th century, changes began. The population was growing, but available farmland was not, and hundreds of thousands of Scandinavians were forced to move to find food or work. Some peasants moved to the new industrial towns that were beginning to develop. They worked in factories and lived in slums. Many died from tuberculosis or cholera. Others migrated across the Atlantic. Many of them were fleeing not only poverty, but also religious persecution. They sailed to North America in search of freedom and food.

It was around then, too, that peasants began to turn away from their local costumes and imitate the fashions they saw in the towns. At the same time, the

The man and woman on the left are in Scandinavian wedding clothes. Their clothes are made of wool, but the woman's blouse was often silk. On the right is a bride and, standing, her matron of honor.

richer Scandinavians began to re-create and reconstruct—or in some cases, create—costumes from the areas in which they were living, although copies were not always accurate.

National Costume

National costume has grown out of folk costume. It became popular at the beginning of the 20th century. The Norwegian national costume is the *bunad*. The style owes its origins to the traditions of folk dancing and folk music.

Those traditions are still strong now, with competitions every year for playing the special folk fiddle, for singing, and for dancing.

There are more than 200 types of *bunader*. Some are 20th-century reconstructions using local and historical materials to help them be as authentic as possible. Others are based on local costumes. Women wear *bunad* with a headdress both indoors and out, and sometimes a coat. They usually wear black stockings and black shoes with silver buckles. Often, they wear silver jewelry, such as a brooch, at the top of the blouse.

Norwegians wear *bunad* on all types of occasions, not just traditional events, such as weddings. They might wear their special costume to a gala or to an official function.

House Painter

Scandinavians built their houses and furniture from wood. They liked painted china and would display their china collections along wooden shelves as decoration. They painted wooden chests and boxes, too, and wove striped rugs for their wooden floors.

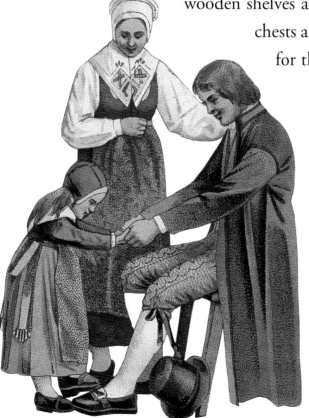

The wild and mountainous Swedish province of Dalarna is famous for preserving old traditions. Folk dress was the same throughout the region. The color of a single item of clothing—an apron, for example—was enough to distinguish one community from another.

Weaving

Weaving was used a lot in Scandinavia, not just to make clothes, but also to produce rugs and wall hangings.

The Scandinavians learned thousands of years ago how to make thread and to weave. They used two sets of threads to weave with. The first set was held in place in long lines on the loom or weaving machine. This was called the warp thread. The second thread was the weft thread. The weft thread was passed across the warp threads, going over and under the warp threads. As each row was finished, weavers pushed the rows of weft thread closely together, and this made cloth. Sometimes, they did extra decorating with dyed threads, or they stitched patterns on with embroidery, or stamped them on.

Finnish women, especially, had beautifully woven aprons. Festive garments were woven from wool with a cotton warp. They usually wove colorful groups of broad stripes. In the 1800s, narrow stripes became popular, influenced—very late—by fashions in towns.

One Swedish artist, Carl Larsson, did a series of famous watercolor paintings of family life in a Swedish farmhouse. The paintings took him almost 10 years and were eventually published as a book, *Ett Hem* (Our Home), in 1899.

Carl Larsson, who was born in 1853, did not have a very happy life until he met his wife and moved to his house at Sundborn. There he lived happily with his wife and seven children, who all appear in the paintings. He shows them at breakfast in the garden, harvesting apples, surprising the maid on her birthday, and all sorts of other occasions.

Larsson drew clothes, furniture, and rooms down to the last tiny detail, and brought to life a vivid picture of what it was like to live in Sweden at that time. He died in 1919.

The Low Countries

Holland, Belgium, and Luxembourg make up the Low Countries. As the name suggests, they are all low-lying. Over the centuries, that has made them easy to invade, and their history has been one of invasion and rule by foreign powers.

The history of Holland has also been one of trading. By the 16th century, Holland had become the world's leading sea power. It was perfectly placed on the European coast for the Dutch—the name for the people who live in Holland—to make the most of their merchanting skills. The port of Amsterdam became one of the biggest, busiest, and richest in Europe. This time was known as Holland's Golden Age.

Dutch merchants traded all over Europe as well as with Asia, South Africa, and the **New World**. They were not only clever, but also cautious and prudent. They bought expensive silks from Persia and sold them to other countries, like France, for even more money. Then the Dutch themselves would buy cheaper woolen cloth from England.

In the panel above, a couple from Zeeland are dressed in their finest for a special occasion. The man below, also from Zeeland, is shown carrying a spade as a symbol of the region's abundance.

The Dutch were known as a sober and pious nation, methodical and steady, solid believers in the home and family and the virtues of hard work.

The Ruff

The Dutch were not a nation to either start or accept new fashion trends. They had none of the flamboyance of the French or Italian courts, nor the stark style of the Spanish. But one fashion they did adopt was the ruff. The ruff first appeared in Europe around the start of the 16th century. From the first modest folds of linen and lace around the neck, it grew bigger and bigger and stiffer and stiffer, with more and more layers.

It was an uncomfortable, restricting type of garment that limited movement and forced its wearers to sit up straight. However, it became a symbol of wealth and status. The more layers a ruff had, the richer you appeared. Only a man with servants could manage the maintenance the ruffs required. Only a man with no need to do any kind of hard physical work could wear one.

By the second half of the 16th century, most other countries had gotten tired of the restrictions of the bigger ruff, and they began to make them smaller. Not the Dutch, however. As the 16th century moved toward the 17th, Dutch ruffs became even bigger. Some were so big they even made it difficult to eat.

The ruff held far less appeal for women than for men. In the first half of the century, old women wore them, but younger ones tended to wear a flat collar. By the middle of the century, older women, too, had abandoned the ruff in favor of the flat collar.

Dutch Style

The Dutch rated comfort far higher than elegance. In the cold of winter, men might wear several vests or pairs of trousers. Dutch clothes overall looked somewhat dull compared with those of many other European countries, and styles changed slowly. The colors were somber: grays, black, brownish yellows, and whites, but rarely red.

Most women, whatever their walk in life, wore aprons over their dresses. Aprons, which came to be regarded as a national emblem, were usually white, black, or violet, and sometimes trimmed with lace. The bodice of a dress varied, but whatever style choices a Dutch woman made, the result was usually severe. Some were cut in a low triangular shape at the front. Some came with sleeves, some without, and some came with false sleeves of different shades. The bodice was usually of a different material and color from the dress. Some had vertical stripes to help give the illusion of height. Women wore at least one petticoat under their dress, and in winter many more.

Religious Splits

By the middle of the 16th century, Holland, Belgium, and Luxembourg were under the rule of Philip II, the Catholic king of Spain. However, by that time, many in the north had become followers of John Calvin, a French Protestant religious reformer. Philip II persecuted and fought the Dutch Protestants. In return, they worshipped more openly and fought more doggedly.

By 1581, the Protestants had attained independence, and only the provinces in the south—modern Belgium and Luxembourg—would be under Spanish rule. The seven Protestant states in the north would rule themselves and be known as the United Provinces. Soon, people began to call the united land Holland, after the richest and most powerful province of the seven states.

The invention of starch at the beginning of the 17th century meant that ruffs could be stiffened and no longer needed a wire frame to hold them in place.

Religious influences can be seen in the plain white collar and the hat style, but ribbons appeared, and bows decorated the shoes. Some adopted the flamboyant fashions of the English Cavaliers, such as bright colors.

Calvinism was a strict and severe religion and it affected fashions in Holland. A typical outfit had a plain white collar and a hooded cape. Long hair for men was frowned upon, as was dancing or any form of exuberance, and at one time, jewelry was considered shameful.

Hats and Caps

In the first years of the 17th century, men wore enormous conical hats with wide, floppy brims turned up in front. Then brims became straight, as did the hat. After that, wide brims returned, but cut in irregular lines.

Ribbons appeared everywhere as trimming and became fashionable on hats, as did feathers. Feathers were dyed in current colors, then curled with a special feather curler made of bone.

Nearly all Dutch women wore caps, both indoors and out. By 1600, embroidered caps hugged the head and hid the ears and nape of the neck. Some time later, the **mobcap** became popular, a style borrowed from the French.

Coats and Cloaks

The dressing gown was a traditional Dutch garment, but men wore it over the doublet like a coat when they went to work or to shop. It was ankle-length and sometimes lined with velvet or fur.

The *huik* (cloak) was a long, tough coat, which featured a tall hood that was kept upright by a stiff rod bent into a semicircle.

The *vlieger* was a long cape that got broader toward the ground. All women wore one in 1600. It was nearly always black and lined with fur, and came either with or without sleeves. By 1640, the *vlieger* was generally out of favor, and only **matrons** wore them.

Inside a Dutch House

Family life was highly important to the Dutch. The family home was where they liked to be. Dutch houses

Painters

In a short space of time during the 17th century, Holland produced an enormous number of famous painters. The most famous of all is perhaps Rembrandt, but there were many others, too: Rubens, Van Dyck, Vermeer, Frans Hals, and more.

The Dutch painters of this time were known throughout Europe and were much in demand as portrait painters at the royal courts. Their realism and ability to convey the precise texture of a piece of clothing make them an invaluable guide to the fashions of the time.

Women in Holland continued to wear caps for a long time. These are from the 19th century, and have particularly fine spiral hairpins with jewelry suspended from them.

were cozy, but not necessarily comfortable. Ceilings were low, windows were small, and stairways were steep. In many houses, each room was on a different level, and going from one room to another meant climbing a number of short stairways.

In many houses at that time, the entrance hall was used as a sitting room, containing a table and a few chairs, a china cupboard, copper cauldrons, and decorative porcelain. In richer homes, the entrance hall became a grander room, with perhaps a marble bench, hunting trophies, and fine pictures.

A cupboard was a sign of wealth and success, two cupboards even more so. One would hold linen, the other china. Poor people made do with old-fashioned lidded chests painted in green and red.

The Dutch were extremely proud of their homes and would even include the sidewalk and roadway in front of the house in their cleaning regime, which was **rigorous**. Some houses used up to 40 buckets of water a day for cleaning. Houses often felt damp, because every bit of wooden furniture, even stairs, benches, and floorboards, would get a good scrubbing. Pans would be polished and furniture waxed. Some richer people had a servant who did nothing but clean all day. With everything kept so spotless, any visitors would usually be given straw slippers to put over their shoes.

Sometimes, people did not use the rooms they were most proud of unless they had visitors. The woman of the house and her daughters and servants might all squash into a small nearby room to sew or knit, instead of using the drawing room. Or, she might have a kitchen full of gleaming copper and pewter and a floor tiled with marble, then cook in a little alcove elsewhere to avoid creating a mess.

In many families, cooking was done only once a week, and all the dishes cooked on that day were reheated on the following days. People ate with their fingers, because spoons were rare. Forks were not used at all until 1700, and even then they were a luxury.

Sweet Dreams

Bedrooms were a new idea in the 17th century, and in many houses, beds might still be part of the sitting room, built into the wall like a cupboard. Some had a lower section with a pullout drawer in which smaller children slept.

In towns, bedrooms were beginning to catch on. Rich people might have a four-poster bed with curtains in the middle of the room, sometimes on a platform. The bed might be carved with the owner's **coat of arms**, garlands and festoons, or satyrs and angels. Sometimes feathers were fastened to the corners.

The beds were not comfortable. The wall beds were so short that people had to sleep almost sitting up. The four-posters had a hard frame and a thick feather bag to sleep on, with piles of pillows, which meant sleeping slightly raised up. A second feather bag as a covering meant that it got hot as well as uncomfortable.

Children and Clothes

In common with the rest of Europe, Dutch children dressed in exactly the same clothes as adults from a young age. Babies were extremely well wrapped up. They wore headdresses, sleeved undershirts, jackets, and woolen robes. Such clothing meant they could hardly move.

Young children wore a burdensome number of clothes, too. Once they could stand, they were put in a wooden chair with a high back and a little table at the front that held them in. Some of these chairs had wheels on them.

Views on what was good for children were different then as well. Fresh air was blocked out as much as possible. Babies slept with closed windows at all times, and under a lot of blankets with a hot water bottle tucked inside.

Flower Power

The Dutch loved flowers, not to cut and put in vases in their homes, but arranged methodically in their gardens. They would group roses, hyacinths, and lilies together, yellow flowers on one side, red on the other.

Every town had its own florist's shop. Demand became so great that the area around Haarlem, which was ideally suited to flower growing, was devoted to the industry, developing and growing new types of flowers to provide to the florists.

Until 1615, roses were the clear favorite. However, in 1593, the tulip, native to Turkey, arrived in Holland. It had a slow, quiet start there, but then two things happened at once: a sudden craze for tulips began in Paris, and a plant disease spread in Dutch gardens that produced strange new patterns and colors on the tulips.

Dutch flower growers were quick to seize the opportunity—and so were the ordinary Dutch people. For a while, madness reigned as new types of bulbs were developed and sold for breathtaking amounts of money. Almost everyone was growing new varieties, from butchers and bakers to tax collectors. People stayed awake all night guarding their flower beds. Some made fortunes and some lost everything, but in the end the business calmed down. The tulip industry had come to stay.

No one thought children needed play clothes. Children were dressed like small adults from a young age. In some villages, boys wore girls' clothes until they were seven.

Some people strapped their children into tightly laced corsets that were made of whalebone, with iron and lead inserts to make them more rigid. They thought it would help the child's bones grow straight. Parents might also make their children wear a tight leather cap to protect them from knocks on the head. By 1620, however, people were beginning to realize that these clothes were cruel. They began to object to the old customs, but it took another 100 years for the practice to die out.

Peasant Style

Throughout the centuries, clothing styles hardly changed at all for Dutch peasants. They did not buy new clothes because fashions had changed; they bought them when the old ones were worn out—and sometimes that might take two or three generations.

Poorer laborers in towns wore simple, old-fashioned clothes in coarse woolen materials, all protected by a leather apron. Typical colors were black, blue, brown, or gray.

All seven provinces had their own variations on the traditional peasant costumes. In every region, there were distinct forms of ornamentation, favored colors, and combinations of accessories.

Glossary

Note: Specialized words relating to clothing are explained within the text, but those that appear more than once are listed below for easy reference.

Amber fossilized resin (a sap from trees), deep yellowish in color

Amulet a protective charm

Beauty spot a tiny piece of black silk or court plaster worn on the face or neck, especially by women, to hide a blemish or to heighten beauty

Bodice the close-fitting upper part, from shoulder to waist, of a woman's dress, which may be separate from or attached to the dress

Bourgeois a member of the middle class, for example, a merchant or shopkeeper

Brooch an ornament that is held by a pin or clasp and is worn at or near the neck

Bustle a frame or pad causing the skirt to stand out from the hips

Cloth of gold cloth woven of threads of gold and silk or wool

Coat of arms the particular heraldic bearings of a person or family, usually depicted with accompanying items (such as a crest, motto, and supporters)

Codpiece a pouch worn by men in the front of tight hose or breeches

Conical cone-shaped

Damask a firm fabric made with flat patterns in a satin weave on a plain-woven background

Doublet a man's close-fitting garment for the upper body

Drawstring a string, cord, or tape inserted into hems laced through eyelets for use in closing a bag or controlling fullness in garments

Fjord long, narrow, rocky inlet

Flock waste parts of wool or cloth

Game wild animals hunted for food or sport

Gauze a thin, often transparent, fabric used chiefly for clothing or draperies

Gorge a narrow steep-walled canyon or part of a canyon

Hose a covering for the legs and feet

Insignia a sign or badge showing a person's office or rank

Jerkin a close-fitting, hip-length, usually sleeveless jacket

Kirtle a skirt and bodice sewn together to make one piece

Matron a married woman, usually marked by dignified maturity or social distinction

Mercenary a soldier hired and paid to fight, sometimes in the service of a foreign king

Mobcap a woman's fancy indoor cap made with a high full crown and often tied under the chin

New World the parts of the world discovered in the 15th and 16th centuries, especially the continents of North and South America

Rigorous having the qualities of difficulty and strictness

Scabbard a holder, or sheath, to put a sword in

Stocks a device for publicly punishing offenders, consisting of a wooden frame with holes in which the feet, or feet and hands, can be locked

Tunic a simple slip-on garment made with or without sleeves and usually knee-length, belted at the waist, and worn as an under or outer garment

Timeline

6 B.C.–A.D. 30 Jesus of Nazareth lives and founds Christianity in Palestine.

A.D. 750 The first raids of the Norsemen begin in Europe.

1096 The First Crusade begins.

1147 The Second Crusade begins.

1189 The Third Crusade begins.

1227 Germany defeats Denmark and begins to expand Baltic trade.

1437 The Hapsburgs of Austria begin their rule of Germany.

1445 The Bible becomes the first printed book in Europe.

1492 Christopher Columbus discovers the West Indies.

1498 Vasco da Gama of Portugal reaches India.

1509 John Calvin is born in France.

1517 Martin Luther begins his attacks on the Catholic Church in Germany.

1568–1648 The Dutch Revolt (a struggle for independence from Spain).

1581 Seven northern Dutch provinces proclaim independence as the United Provinces.

1600–1675 The "Golden Age" of Holland.

1618–1648 The Thirty Years War between Protestants and Catholics.

1643–1645 War between Sweden and Denmark leaves Sweden the major power in the Baltic.

1661 First European banknote issued in Sweden.

1740–1786 Frederick II, "the Great," rules Prussia in Germany.

1767 James Hargreaves invents the spinning jenny, the first successful spinning machine, in Great Britain.

1775 James Watt invents the steam engine in Great Britain.

1789 The French Revolution begins.

1871 The king of Prussia becomes emperor of a united Germany.

1905 Norway becomes independent from Sweden.

1919 Finland is declared a republic.

Online Sources

The Costumer's Manifesto
www.costumes.org
A great starting point for further research. This site offers a wide range of information and links on costume throughout the ages.

The Costume Page
http://members.aol.com/nebula5/costume.html
A library of costume and costuming-related links with over 2,000 links listed on these pages.

Costume Through the Centuries
www.milieux.com/costume/costume1.html
An excellent site that gives students a good starting point for further independent research.

Early Renaissance Fashion Terms
http://www.furman.edu/~kgossman/history/earlyren/terms.htm
Part of the "Brief History of Fashion" site, these excellent pages give clear, concise definitions of Renaissance fashion terms. Images, links, and a timeline provide additional clarification.

Further Reading

Clare, John D. *I Was There: Vikings*. London: Bodley Head Children's Books, 1991.

Cumming, Valerie. *Exploring Costume History 1500–1900*. London: Batsford, 1981.

Elliot, D. *Europe's History*. Hove, England: Wayland, 1994.

Huggett, Frank E. *Netherlands: The Land and Its People*. London: Macdonald Educational, 1976.

Kelly, Francis M. and Randolph Schwabe. *European Costume and Fashion 1490–1790*. Mineola, NY: Dover, 2002.

Laver, James. *Costume and Fashion*. London: Thames and Hudson, 1995.

Peacock, John. *Costume: 1066–1990s*. London: Thames and Hudson, 1986.

Ribeiro, Aileen. *Dress in Eighteenth-Century Europe 1715–1789* (revised ed.). New Haven, Connecticut: Yale University Press, 2002.

Salariya, David. *Vikings and Their Travels*. Hemel Hempstead, England: Simon and Schuster, 1993.

Stibbert, Frederic. *European Civil and Military Clothing: From the First to the Eighteenth Century*. Mineola, NY: Dover, 2001.

Wingate, Philippa. *The Viking World*. London: Usborne, 1994.

About the Author

Emma Fischel has been writing books for children for more than 10 years. Published non-fiction includes 13 titles in the highly successful series of biographies for Franklin Watts, for ages six to nine years. The biographies explain the lives of famous people with a wealth of extra detail about their lives and times and the culture that shaped them.

Other subjects have ranged widely: from inventors (Alexander Graham Bell and George Stephenson), to explorers (Captain Scott), to writers (William Shakespeare, Roald Dahl, Hans Christian Andersen), to politicians, statesmen, and other key figures of their time (Julius Caesar, Mahatma Gandhi, Boudicca, Francis Drake, Emmeline Pankhurst, and Saint Francis.)

As well as further non-fiction titles she has also had published eight fiction books, with an age range of 3 to 13 years.

Index